National Audit Office

Department of Health & Social Care

Investigation into NHS spending on generic medicines in primary care

Report by the Comptroller and Auditor General

Ordered by the House of Commons
to be printed on 6 June 2018

This report has been prepared under Section 6 of the National Audit Act 1983 for presentation to the House of Commons in accordance with Section 9 of the Act

Sir Amyas Morse KCB
Comptroller and Auditor General
National Audit Office

4 June 2018

HC 1122 | £10.00

This investigation sets out the facts in relation to the increase in costs to the NHS of certain generic medicines in primary care in 2017-18.

Investigations

We conduct investigations to establish the underlying facts in circumstances where concerns have been raised with us, or in response to intelligence that we have gathered through our wider work.

006274 06/18 NAO

Contents

The National Audit Office study team consisted of:
Sergiu Cociu, Natalie Low, Elisabeth Moore and Will Palmer, with assistance from Andrew Bax, Matt Beaumont and Ben Wade, under the direction of Robert White.

This report can be found on the National Audit Office website at www.nao.org.uk

For further information about the National Audit Office please contact:

National Audit Office
Press Office
157–197 Buckingham Palace Road
Victoria
London
SW1W 9SP

Tel: 020 7798 7400

Enquiries: www.nao.org.uk/contact-us

Website: www.nao.org.uk

Twitter: @NAOorguk

Key facts

£3.5bn
estimated amount the NHS spent on generic medicines in primary care in 2016-17, including a target £800 million contribution to pharmacies

709
number of price concessions that the Department of Health & Social Care (the Department) granted in 2017-18, up from 282 in 2016-17

£315m
National Audit Office estimate of the net spend on concessionary priced medicines in primary care in 2017-18 (over and above the amount that would have been paid via lower Drug Tariff prices)

Seven times the increase between the net spend on price concessions for generic medicines in primary care in 2017-18, compared with 2016-17

81% proportion of spending on generic medicines that is in primary care, 2016-17

3,000 number of concessionary pricing requests made by pharmacists in November 2017; before May 2017, the monthly figure was fewer than 150 requests

£800 million agreed annual margin retained by pharmacies as part of their funding to provide NHS pharmacy services. This is the difference between the price at which a pharmacy purchases a medicine and the price that the NHS reimburses the pharmacy when the medicine is dispensed.

Glossary of key terms

'Generic' and 'branded' medicines – New medicines, generally marketed under their brand name, have patents that are protected for a minimum of 20 years. During this time, no other company can manufacture or market the medicine. At the end of this time-period other companies can manufacture and market the same medicine under its generic name, typically selling it at a lower price.

Drug Tariff price – Each month the Department publishes the Drug Tariff. This sets out what pharmacies in primary care will be reimbursed for the cost of each generic medicine they dispense for an NHS prescription.

Concessionary prices – If pharmacies in primary care cannot purchase a medicine at, or under, the Drug Tariff price, the Department can set a higher 'concessionary' reimbursement price for that month.

What this investigation is about

1 During 2017, the prices of certain medicines purchased by pharmacies for the NHS increased unexpectedly. This placed what NHS England described as a "significant unbudgeted pressure" on clinical commissioning groups. In 2017-18, the net spend on the affected medicines totalled an estimated £315 million, nearly seven times greater than the equivalent spend in 2016-17. During 2017-18, the costs of certain individual medicines increased more than tenfold.

2 The medicines affected by these price increases were 'generic' medicines. Medicines can be 'branded' or 'generic'. Branded medicines are medicines sold under the name given by the company that made them. New medicines have patents that are protected for a minimum of 20 years, and are generally marketed under their brand name. During that time, no other company can manufacture or market the medicine. At the end of this period, other companies can manufacture and market the medicine under its generic name, typically selling it at a lower price. In 2016-17, the NHS spent an estimated £4.3 billion, or 28% of total medicine expenditure, on generic medicines.

3 This investigation sets out the facts in relation to:

- NHS spending on generic medicines, and the 2017-18 increase in spending on certain generic medicines;
- possible causes of the price increases in the market for generic medicines; and
- how the Department of Health & Social Care (the Department) and its arm's-length bodies responded to the price increases.

4 This investigation focuses on primary care, where most spending on generic medicines is incurred. It is intended to be the first report in a wider programme of work on medicines.

Summary

Key findings

The increase in prices of certain generic medicines

1 **The NHS spent an estimated £4.3 billion on generic medicines in 2016-17, of which most was spent in primary care.** In 2016-17, the spend on generic medicines in primary care was £3.5 billion.[1] In primary care, pharmacies buy medicines from wholesalers or manufacturers who determine their own prices. The Department of Health & Social Care (the Department) does not set the price of generic medicines. Instead the Department reimburses pharmacies set amounts for the medicines they dispense, which are published in the Drug Tariff. If pharmacies cannot get a medicine at this set amount, the Department can use a mechanism called concessionary prices. This allows it to reimburse pharmacies at a temporarily higher price than the Drug Tariff price (paragraphs 1.2 and 1.8).

2 **The prices of certain generic medicines increased unexpectedly in 2017-18.** There was an unprecedented increase in the number of requests from pharmacies for concessionary prices. These increased from fewer than 150 a month before May 2017 to a peak of 3,000 in November 2017. In 2017-18, the Department granted 709 concessionary prices, up from 282 in 2016-17 (paragraphs 2.1 and 2.2).

3 **The price increases resulted in additional unforeseen costs for clinical commissioning groups.** Clinical commissioning groups are ultimately responsible for expenditure on medicines for their patient population. We estimated the net spend on concessionary priced medicines at £315 million in 2017-18 (that is, over and above what would have been spent if the Drug Tariff price applied). This was seven times greater than the equivalent spend in 2016-17. Ten medicines accounted for around half of this net spend. The cost of certain medicines increased more than tenfold: for example, at its peak, the concessionary price for Quetiapine 100mg tablets was £113.10, 70 times higher than its previous set price of £1.59. In October 2017, NHS England began forecasting an end-of-year overspend across clinical commissioning groups, partly due to the issues in the generics market. In May 2018, NHS England reported an unaudited end-of-year deficit of around £250 million among clinical commissioning groups (paragraphs 2.3 to 2.6).

1 This includes an agreed £800 million contribution to pharmacies.

Causes of price increases

4 **The Department identified three main factors that may have caused the price increases but cannot fully verify or quantify these.** These include the suspension of some manufacturers' licences and a fall in the value of sterling. Our analysis indicates that the Department identified a direct relationship between price increases and shortages for four out of 10 medicines subject to concessionary pricing in October 2017. (paragraphs 3.7 to 3.9).

5 **Analysis by the Department in November 2017 identified unexpected increases in wholesalers' margins.** The Department undertook analysis to understand what was happening in the market. It identified increases in manufacturers' prices, but also unexpected increases in wholesalers' margins in 2017, which it could not fully explain. The NHS will not be able to get back the expenditure due to the increase in manufacturer and wholesaler prices. The Department's analysis also showed that the concessionary prices it had granted were set higher than necessary above wholesalers' selling prices. It estimated that this amounted to £86.3 million of additional costs for clinical commissioning groups in 2017-18, which it expects to be recouped in subsequent years through the established reimbursement mechanisms. The Department subsequently changed its calculation of concessionary prices, basing this on manufacturers' rather than wholesalers' prices (paragraphs 3.10 and 3.11).

How the Department and its arm's-length bodies responded to the price increases

6 **The Department told us it took action to maintain the supply of those generic medicines on concessionary prices for patients in 2017-18.** The Department is responsible for ensuring the supply of medicines. Its actions included: liaising with manufacturers to identify whether supplies were available; permitting one manufacturer whose licence was suspended to supply certain medicines considered critical and releasing supplies of one medicine from a centrally held stockpile (paragraph 3.3).

7 **The Department received intelligence from a variety of sources about potential impacts of the price increases.** This included information about how supply issues were affecting pharmacies' ability to obtain medicines, although the Department does not know how many patients experienced problems getting their prescriptions. We also heard concerns from the Pharmaceutical Services Negotiating Committee about the impact of price increases on its sector (paragraphs 3.4 and 3.5).

8 **The Department will have new powers to control the price of generic medicines, which are due to come into force from July 2018.** Following some high-profile cases of issues with the price of some generic medicines (before 2017-18), new legislation has strengthened the Department's powers to control the price of generic medicines. The legislation also introduced mandatory information-sharing arrangements. Before July 2018, the Department had to rely on voluntary arrangements, which limited its ability to identify and respond to the recent price increases. However, its new powers are untested and will require sufficient resources (paragraphs 3.12 to 3.15).

Part One

NHS spending on generic medicines

Introduction

1.1 Medicines purchased by the NHS can be 'branded' or 'generic'. New medicines, generally marketed under their brand name, have patents that are protected for a minimum of 20 years. During this time, no other company can manufacture or market the medicine. This protection is intended to provide pharmaceutical companies with an opportunity to earn a return on their research and development investment, and provide incentives for them to develop new medicines. At the end of this period, other companies can manufacture and market the same medicine under its generic name, typically selling it at a lower price.

1.2 In 2016-17, the NHS spent an estimated £4.3 billion on generic medicines across hospital, community and primary care settings, such as general practice.[2] This accounted for 28% of the total spend on medicines (**Figure 1**). The majority, some 81% or £3.5 billion, of spending on generic medicines was in primary care. Common medicines used in primary care include those used to lower cholesterol (statins) and treat indigestion and high blood pressure, and painkillers such as aspirin and paracetamol.

1.3 The generic medicines market is global. The Medicines and Healthcare products Regulatory Agency reports that the value of the UK generic medicines market was estimated to be 2.6% of the global market in 2016. It also reports that globally 20% of exported generic medicines come from India. While it is difficult to make exact international comparisons, research suggests that the prices of generic medicines in the UK may be lower than in comparator countries. The UK's use of generic medicines is also comparatively high, both in terms of value and the volume of medicines dispensed.

2 Primary care spend on generic medicines includes an agreed £800 million contribution to pharmacies.

Figure 1

The Department of Health & Social Care's estimates of spending on branded and generic medicines in primary and secondary care, 2016-17

28% of the total NHS spend on medicines was on generic medicines

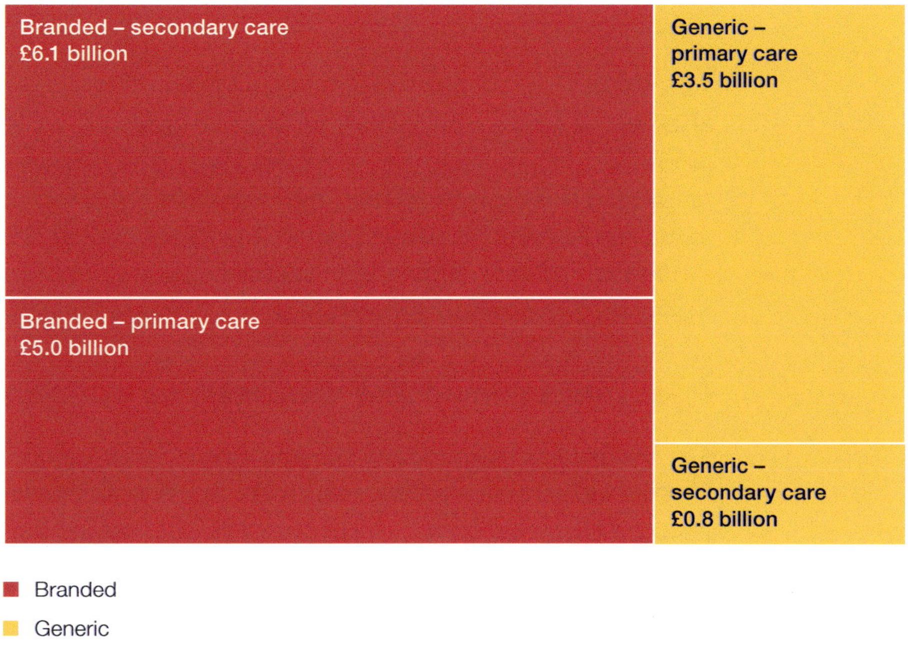

Notes

1 Figures as provided by the Department.

2 Primary care spend on generic medicines includes an agreed £800 million contribution to pharmacies.

3 For secondary care the proportion of spend on branded versus generic medicines is based on an estimated 88% and 12% split respectively.

Source: Department of Health & Social Care

Roles and responsibilities

1.4 The Department of Health & Social Care (the Department) recognises that it has a role to play in creating and maintaining a competitive, vibrant and sustainable market for generic medicines in the UK and ensuring the availability of generic medicines via a resilient supply chain that provides a reasonable financial return for all parties. NHS England's shared responsibility for balancing the NHS budget includes budgetary responsibility for spending on medicines in primary care. The Medicines and Healthcare products Regulatory Agency is responsible for ensuring medicines are safe and grants licences for products, manufacturers and wholesalers.

1.5 NHS England allocates money to clinical commissioning groups for local expenditure on medicines. Clinical commissioning groups can seek to influence cost-effective prescribing behaviours through, for example, issuing guidance but do not have statutory powers over prescribers. Prescribing decisions rest with clinicians such as GPs who do not pay for the medicines they prescribe.[3] Pharmacists dispense the medicine as written on the prescription form and these costs flow through to clinical commissioning group budgets.

1.6 Getting best value from medicines and pharmacies is part of the NHS's 10-point efficiency plan, as set out in the *Next Steps on the NHS Five Year Forward View*. The NHS also continues to target generic medicines for further savings by increasing generic prescribing and dispensing rates. In primary care, the proportion of total spending on medicines that was made up of generic medicines increased from 30% to 41% between 2010-11 and 2016-17 (**Figure 2**). In the last two years of that period, the volume of generic medicines dispensed continued to increase, although the average price reduced.

Price management and concessionary pricing

1.7 **Figure 3** on page 12 sets out how the prices of generic medicines are managed. Pharmacies purchase generic medicines directly from the market, which determines the price for these medicines.[4] The Department does not set the price of generic medicines. Instead it sets the amount pharmacies will be reimbursed for generic medicines and relies on competition in the market to control price. The Department estimates that, in 2017, there were fewer than 100 wholesalers regularly selling generic medicines in the UK and some 100 or so manufacturers of generic medicines.

1.8 Each month the Department publishes the Drug Tariff, which sets out what pharmacies will be reimbursed for the cost of each generic medicine they dispense for an NHS prescription. On occasion pharmacies may find they cannot purchase a medicine at, or under, the Drug Tariff price. In this situation, pharmacies can submit a report to the Pharmaceutical Services Negotiating Committee, to request reimbursement at a temporarily higher 'concessionary' price (Figure 3). The Pharmaceutical Services Negotiating Committee may then request that the Department grants a concessionary price for that medicine for that month. Between April 2017 and March 2018, on average the Department granted more than nine out of 10 requests for a concessionary price.

3 With the exception of dispensing GPs, who can prescribe and dispense medicines.
4 Pharmacies include independent pharmacies and pharmacy chains and, for this report, dispensing GPs (see footnote 3).

Figure 2

The Department of Health & Social Care's estimate of spend on generic and branded medicines dispensed in primary care

The proportion of medicine spend on generics in primary care increased between 2010-11 and 2016-17

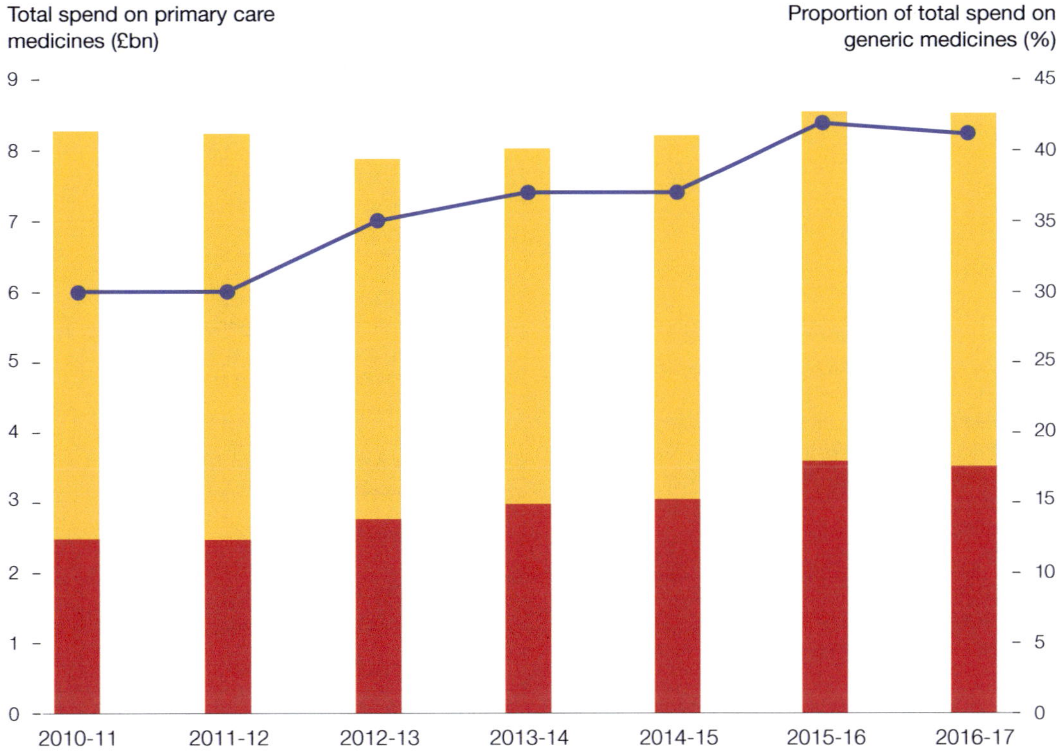

	2010-11	2011-12	2012-13	2013-14	2014-15	2015-16	2016-17
■ Total spend on generic medicines (£bn)	2.5	2.5	2.8	3.0	3.0	3.6	3.5
■ Total spend on branded medicines (£bn)	5.8	5.8	5.1	5.1	5.2	5.0	5.0
● Proportion of total spend on generic medicines (%)	30	30	35	37	37	42	41

Notes

1 Figures as provided by the Department.

2 Primary care spend on generic medicines includes an agreed £800 million contribution to pharmacies.

Source: National Audit Office analysis of NHS Business Services Authority data

Figure 3

Managing the price of generic medicines in primary care

The market sets the price of generic medicines and reimbursement for pharmacy contractors is set out in the Drug Tariff

Department of Health & Social Care

Responsible for setting the Drug Tariff and the Community Pharmacy Contractual Framework.

Drug Tariff is published monthly and sets out what the NHS pays community pharmacies for providing NHS pharmacy services. This includes how much pharmacies are reimbursed for the cost of medicines.

The reimbursement price of generic medicines, determined by the Secretary of State, is set out in Part VIIIA and includes the following categories.

Category A medicines which are readily available as generic.

Prices are updated monthly.

Category C medicines which are not readily available as generic.

Prices are updated monthly.

Category M medicines which are readily available as generic.

Prices are updated quarterly.

NHS Business Services Authority

Provides information to the Department on price and availability of medicines for requested **concessions** and assists with the data collection for the **Margin Survey**.

How generic reimbursement prices are set

Reimbursement prices are based on a weighted average of prices from two manufacturers and two wholesalers (with greater weight given to the wholesalers' prices).

Reimbursement prices are based on the price for a particular proprietary product, manufacturer or sometimes supplier.

Reimbursement prices are based on information submitted by manufacturers.

These prices may also be adjusted to deliver the pharmacies' margin – set out in the Community Pharmacy Contractual Framework, allowing the sector to retain £800 million ('retained margin'[1]).

Pharmaceutical Services Negotiating Committee

Promotes and supports the interests of community pharmacies in England. Its role includes collating reports of concession pricing requests and, based on these, submitting requests to the Department for concessionary pricing.

How prices may be further adjusted

Margin Survey – one function of the survey is to determine whether Category M prices have delivered pharmacies' 'retained margin'[1], based on invoices of a sample of independent pharmacies.

Category M prices may then be adjusted, upwards to reimburse pharmacies if the margin has not been delivered or downwards if the amount exceeded the margin.

Concessionary pricing and No Cheaper Stock Obtainable – Where pharmacy contractors are unable to purchase a medicine at, or under, the Drug Tariff price, they can submit a concessionary pricing request or a No Cheaper Stock Obtainable (NCSO) report to the Pharmaceutical Services Negotiating Committee – who may then request a price concession from the Department. If accepted, a new concessionary price is applied, and the Drug Tariff price suspended. If a NCSO is accepted contractors are reimbursed the actual price they paid.

These arrangements apply to the specified month only.

Note

1 The 'retained margin' is the difference between the price at which a pharmacy purchases a medicine and the price the pharmacy is reimbursed by the NHS when the medicine is dispensed. Pharmacies receive this as part of their funding to provide NHS pharmacy services.

Source: National Audit Office

1.9 Under the current funding arrangements, pharmacies retain a 'medicines margin' of £800 million a year, the target amount since 2014-15 (see Figure 3 for full details). The margin is the difference between the price that pharmacies purchase medicines at and the amount they are reimbursed. The medicines margin is intended to give an incentive for pharmacies to purchase cost-effectively for the NHS. The Department monitors whether the margin is achieved through an annual survey and adjusts the reimbursement arrangement for following years, as necessary. This involves increasing or decreasing the reimbursement prices of some generic medicines in the following year to recoup any overspends or reimburse any underspends related to the margin from previous years.

Part Two

Price increases during 2017-18

Concessionary pricing and increases in spend during 2017-18

2.1 The number of concessionary pricing requests from pharmacies to the Pharmaceutical Services Negotiating Committee started to increase in May 2017, from fewer than 150 requests a month before May to more than 1,500 between August and December. The number of requests, which includes multiple reporting of the same medicines, peaked at more than 3,000 in November.[5]

2.2 In 2017-18, the Department of Health & Social Care (the Department) granted 709 price concessions, up from 282 in 2016-17 and an unprecedented increase since the scheme started in 2012. The Department started to increase the monthly number of price concessions granted from June 2017, peaking at 91 in November (**Figure 4**).

2.3 We calculated the financial impact of the price concessions as the net spend. The net spend is the difference between the total spend on generic medicines on price concessions and the spend that would have been incurred for those medicines if the previous (lower) Drug Tariff price applied. In 2017-18, the net spend on concessionary medicines reached an estimated £315 million, seven times greater than the net spend in 2016-17 (**Figure 5** on page 16).[6] The monthly net spend increased from £2 million in April 2017 to £53 million in October; by March 2018 the monthly figure was £8 million.

5 Requests from different pharmacies for the same medicine are counted individually, as are requests for a different dosage variation of a medicine.

6 The Department calculates a different estimate of the financial impact in 2017-18, which was £200 million. It includes the net spend but makes subsequent adjustments that the National Audit Office (NAO) estimate does not take into account. The Department subtracts the net spend in previous years. It also reduces its estimate by around £80 million to take account of money it expects clinical commissioning groups to recoup in future years due to an identified gap between wholesalers' selling prices and concessionary prices (see paragraph 3.10). NHS England also produces its own estimate of the "pressure from price concessions", using a similar approach to the NAO.

Figure 4

Number of price concessions for generic medicines granted by the Department of Health & Social Care

The number of price concessions increased significantly during the second half of 2017

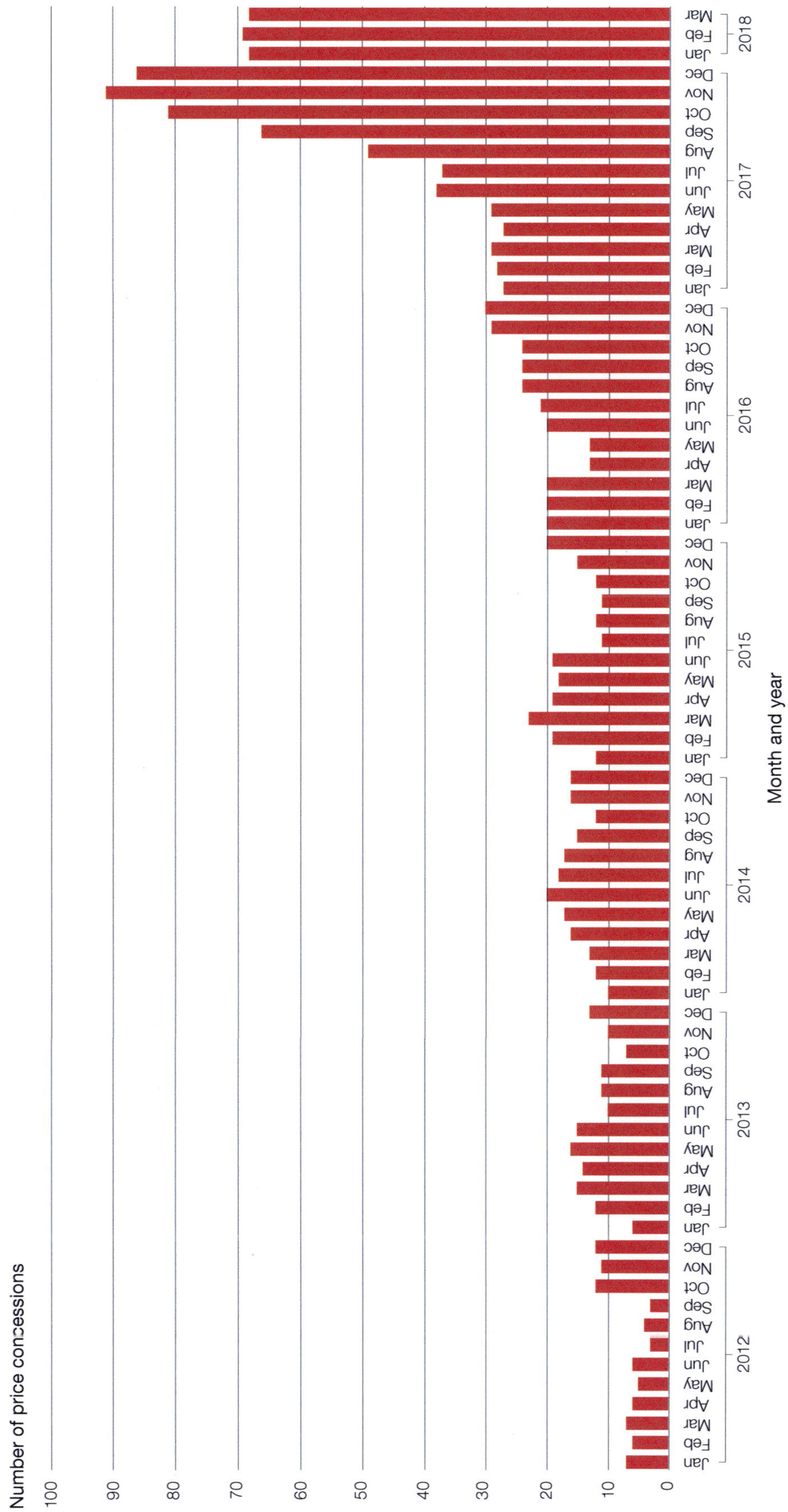

Note

1 Figures include 'No Cheaper Stock Obtainable' concessions (see Figure 3), which the Department last granted in April 2013.

Source: Pharmaceutical Services Negotiating Committee

Figure 5

Estimate of the net spend on price concessions for generic medicines

In 2017-18, the net spend on concessionary medicines was seven times greater than the net spend in 2016-17

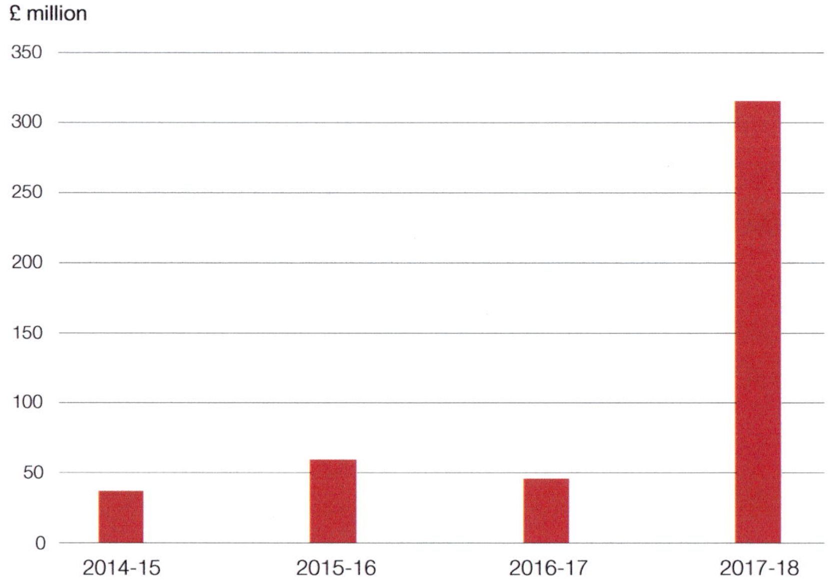

	2014-15	2015-16	2016-17	2017-18
Net spend on concession	37	60	46	315

Note

1 Net spend is the difference between the concession price and Drug Tariff price for a month multiplied by the number of medicines dispensed. Estimates exclude spending in secondary care.

Source: National Audit Office analysis of data from NHS Business Services Authority and OpenPrescribing.net, EBM DataLab, University of Oxford

2.4 Ten medicines accounted for £134 million (43%) of the net spend on price concessions in 2017-18 (**Figure 6**). These medicines are used to treat a range of conditions, including high blood pressure and mental health conditions. During 2017-18, the price of certain individual medicines increased more than tenfold. For example, at its peak, the concession price for Quetiapine 100mg tablets was £113.10, 70 times higher than its previous set price of £1.59.

Figure 6

Medicines with the largest net spend on price concessions in 2017-18

Ten medicines accounted for £134 million of the net spend on price concessions

Medicine name	Estimated net spend (£m)	Drug Tariff price before concession (£)	Peak concessionary price (£)	Percentage change (%)
Amlodipine 5mg	18	0.67	3.75	460
Gabapentin 300mg	17	2.62	13.95	432
Sumatriptan 50mg	16	1.34	31.85	2,277
Levetiracetam 500mg	14	2.48	49.32	1,889
Olanzapine 10mg	14	1.07	69.92	6,435
Quetiapine 100mg	12	1.59	113.10	7,013
Quetiapine 25mg	12	1.03	40.50	3,832
Mefenamic acid 500mg	12	5.80	59.99	934
Amlodipine 10mg	10	0.70	3.99	470
Levetiracetam 1g	9	5.49	95.34	1,637
Total	**134**			

Note

1 Common uses for these medicines are as follows: Amlodipine to treat high blood pressure, Gabapentin to treat epilepsy and nerve pain, Sumatriptan to treat migraines, Levetiracetam to treat epilepsy, Olanzapine and Quetiapine are used to treat schizophrenia and bi-polar disorder and Mefenamic acid to treat pain and inflammation.

Source: National Audit Office analysis of data from NHS Business Services Authority and OpenPrescribing.net, EBM DataLab, University of Oxford

Notification of the financial impact of issues in the generics market

2.5 While the Department, as the policy lead for medicines, manages the concessionary pricing process, NHS England has budgetary responsibility. NHS England was first alerted to the increasing price of certain generic medicines by some clinical commissioning groups in July 2017. In September, NHS England informed the Department of the financial impact on clinical commissioning groups and in its financial report for that month highlighted the growing pressure of concessions on clinical commissioning groups. Its reports for October onwards directly linked the issues in the market for generic medicines with forecast overspends by clinical commissioning groups. It described these issues as a "significant unbudgeted pressure".

2.6 NHS England also began forecasting additional costs for clinical commissioning groups from October 2017 onwards, arising from the increase in concessionary pricing. These forecasts did not take account of changes in wider spending on primary care medicines. For example, in September 2017 NHS England reported that it was unclear whether the pressures from concessionary pricing would ultimately lead to a higher than expected spend on primary care medicines. In May 2018, NHS England reported an unaudited end-of-year deficit among clinical commissioning groups, partly attributed to the concessionary pricing increases, of around £250 million.[7]

7 This £250 million deficit takes account of the release of £440 million of reserves at year-end.

Part Three

Response to and causes of the increase in concessionary prices

The Department's powers to manage supply

3.1 If there are issues with the supply of medicines, the Department of Health & Social Care (the Department), together with the Medicines and Healthcare products Regulatory Agency, can take action to help manage this. Possible actions include:

- getting critical medicines to the market more quickly, for example by speeding up the time taken to grant or change a product licence;
- liaising with companies to help manage supply;
- identifying sources of medicines from abroad, and speeding up importation for individual patients' use; and
- identifying NHS manufacturing units that could meet demand.

3.2 At the time of the concessionary price increases, the Department relied on voluntary arrangements to obtain information from manufacturers, wholesalers and dispensers. Under two voluntary schemes, covering 26 manufacturers or wholesalers in 2017, members submitted quarterly returns to the Department. These included information on costs and volumes of transactions. There were also voluntary guidelines under which companies notified the Department if they were anticipating medicine shortages that might affect patient care.

Management of supply

3.3 The Department told us that its first priority is to ensure sufficient supply of medicines to patients. In relation to the medicines on concessionary prices in 2017-18 it carried out a number of actions:

- The Department contacted manufacturers to identify whether supplies were available and if they could increase supply to the UK when a manufacturer with a large market share for one medicine exited the market without informing the Department.
- In conjunction with the Medicines and Healthcare products Regulatory Agency, the Department permitted one manufacturer whose licence was suspended to supply a medicine considered critical.[8] It also fast-tracked the approval of a change to some manufacturers' licences to supply three other medicines.
- The Department also holds an Essential Medicines Buffer Stockpile and released one cancer medicine affected by concessionary pricing from this stockpile. The Department lists around 500 different medicines for the stockpile, which can be released in the event of a pandemic or other health emergency likely to affect the supply of medicines in the UK. However, during its most recent procurement exercise it procured less than half of the medicines on the list.
- In October 2017, the Department began providing updates for clinical commissioning groups on existing and new supply issues.

3.4 The Department received intelligence from a variety of sources about how supply issues were affecting pharmacies' ability to obtain medicines. It does not know how many patients experienced problems with getting their prescriptions.

3.5 We also heard concerns from the Pharmaceutical Services Negotiating Committee about the impact of the price concessions on pharmacies. It highlighted that the timing of the concessionary prices coincided with reductions in the amount of funding pharmacies receive for payments for services.[9] Funding reduced from £2.8 billion in 2015-16 to £2.6 billion in 2017-18. It also reported greater uncertainty in the sector, with pharmacies having to dispense more medicines above the Drug Tariff price without knowing whether they will be reimbursed the higher price. In December 2017 the Committee reported that most pharmacies were having to work harder than usual to obtain certain medicines.

3.6 In February 2018, NHS England advised clinical commissioning groups to assume, for planning purposes, that the current high level of concessionary pricing would not persist in 2018-19. As set out in paragraph 2.3, the monthly net spend on concessions decreased to £8 million in March 2018, from the peak of £53 million in October. If cost pressures were to continue in 2018-19, the Department would have to decide how any additional unbudgeted costs would be covered.

8 Product licences are granted based on considerations of quality, safety and the efficacy of the medicine.
9 This does not include reimbursements to pharmacies for the cost of medicines, although it does take into account the £800 million 'medicines margin' (see paragraph 1.9).

Underlying causes

3.7 The immediate cause of concessionary pricing is pharmacies being unable to purchase a generic medicine at, or below, the Drug Tariff price. Prices of medicines may be affected by a range of supply-related and other factors. **Figure 7** overleaf sets out the possible causes of the price increases in 2017-18, as reported to us by stakeholders.

3.8 To investigate the underlying causes of the price increases, the Department had to rely on its then voluntary information-sharing arrangements (paragraph 3.2). It also asked its chief commercial officer to investigate in November 2017. The Department identified three main underlying causes of the 2017-18 increase in concessionary pricing:

- the Medicines and Healthcare products Regulatory Agency and European regulators partially suspending the licences of three manufacturers of generic medicines;
- a fall in the value of sterling; and
- governments and insurers in other countries putting downward pressure on the price of generic medicines, resulting in lower returns and manufacturers withdrawing from some markets or medicines: the reduced capacity and competition then increased prices within the UK market.

3.9 The Department was unable to fully verify, or quantify, the relative impact of these three causes, or the other potential causes it considered. We reviewed the Department's assessment of supply issues for the medicines affected by concessionary pricing in October 2017. Our review indicated that the Department identified supply issues for four out of 10 of the medicines affected, accounting for 17% of prescriptions for these medicines.[10] For about half of these medicines, the Department identified the reason for the supply issues, including regulatory action against manufacturers or suppliers exiting the market. The Department had to rely on voluntary arrangements to obtain market information at this time. It had identified that a lack of transparency from these arrangements could lead to "gaming/manipulation of [...] pricing" or "collusion" between organisations in the supply chain. The Department did not identify that this type of behaviour influenced the 2017-18 price increases. However, its ability to rule this out would have been limited.

10 In this context, supply issues include recent, current or intermittent issues.

Figure 7

Possible causes of the generic medicine price increases in 2017-18, as reported by stakeholders

Stakeholders reported a range of supply-related and other factors which may have driven the 2017 price increases

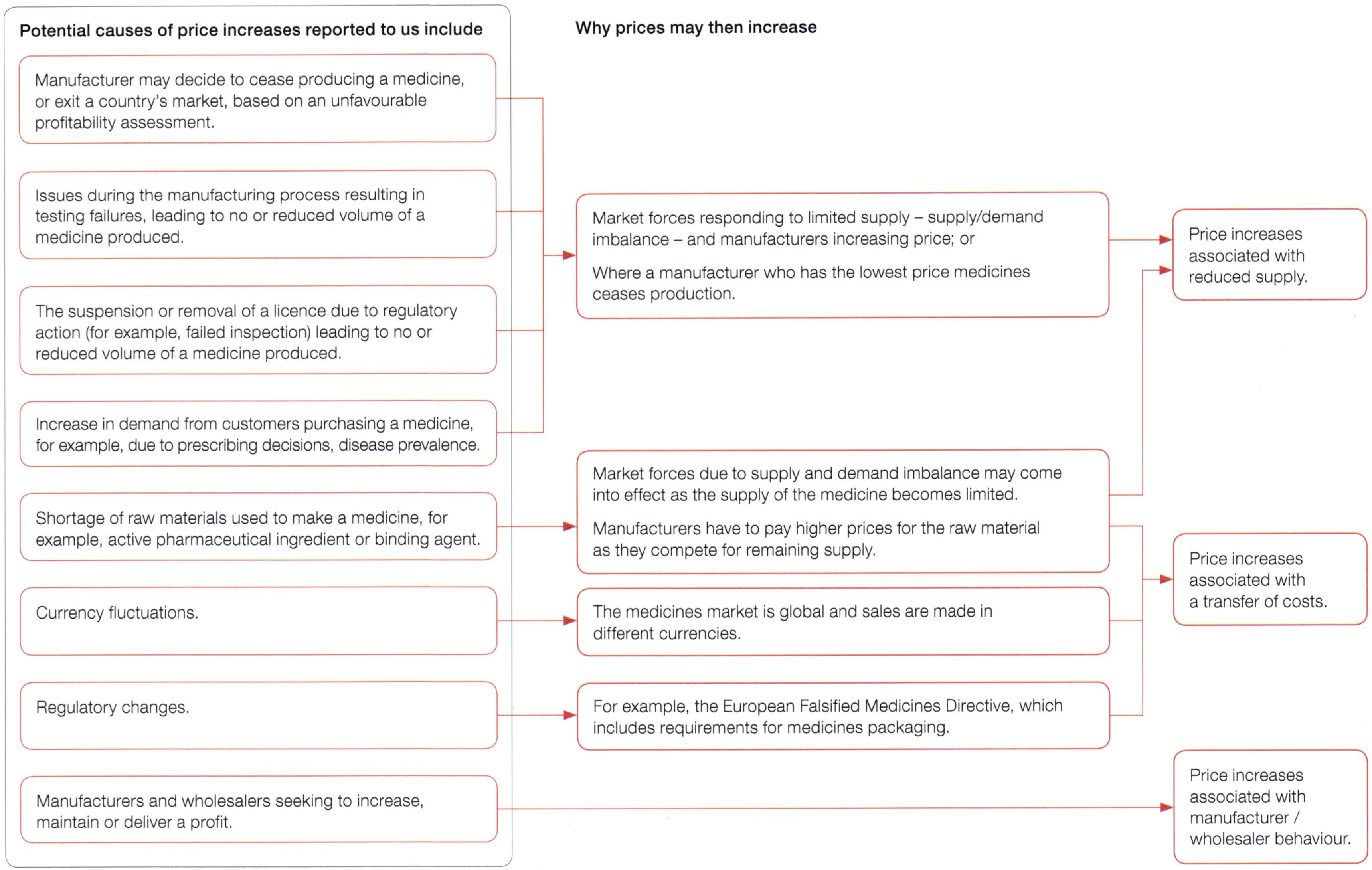

Source: National Audit Office, based on interviews with stakeholders and a review of documents

3.10 The Department told us that its analysis in November 2017 showed that the market for generic medicines had been quite stable until summer 2017. Subsequently, it identified that:

- manufacturers' selling prices increased, which it attributed to the reasons set out in paragraph 3.8;
- the margin between wholesalers' buying and selling prices also unexpectedly increased; and
- there was a gap between wholesalers' selling prices and concessionary prices, meaning the prices it granted were higher than necessary. It estimated that between June and November 2017 this amounted to £86.3 million, which would have been incurred by clinical commissioning groups in 2017-18.

3.11 The Department could not fully explain the reasons for the increase in wholesalers' margins. The NHS will not be able to get back the expenditure due to the increase in manufacturer and wholesaler prices. However, the Department does expect to recoup any overpayment on concessionary prices that were set above wholesalers' prices, through the established mechanism to adjust reimbursement prices to pharmacies in subsequent years (paragraph 1.9). The Department told us that, in November 2017, it changed the way it calculated concessionary prices, basing these on manufacturers' prices, which reduced the concessionary prices it granted.

The Department's new powers

3.12 The supply and concessionary pricing issues happened at a time when there were ongoing concerns about the generics market. The Competition and Markets Authority has investigated instances of suspected anti-competitive behaviour by generic medicines suppliers, including suspected cases of excessive and unfair pricing.[11] Since 2016, it has issued two statements of objections, and one infringement decision (which is on appeal) of suspected cases of excessive pricing (**Figure 8** overleaf).[12] These include cases where companies had allegedly de-branded a medicine, making it generic and no longer subject to price regulation, and then used their market dominance to increase prices unfairly. The Competition and Markets Authority told us that it also has a number of active cases which involve suspected anti-competitive behaviour by pharmaceutical companies, relating to generic medicines.

3.13 The Health Service Medical Supplies (Costs) Act 2017 is intended to address such instances of excessive and unfair pricing of generic medicines. Previously, the National Health Services Act 2006 gave the Secretary of State the power to control the price of generic medicines, but not if the company was a member of the voluntary pricing scheme for branded medicines. The 2017 Act removes this exemption.

11 The Competition and Markets Authority is a non-ministerial department that works to promote competition for the benefit of consumers.
12 Statements of objections set out provisional infringement findings, but do not necessarily lead to an infringement decision.

Figure 8

Competition and Markets Authority's recent suspected cases of excessive and unfair pricing of generic medicines

Since 2016, the Competition and Markets Authority has issued two statements of objections and one infringement decision relating to suppliers of generic medicines

Medicine	Extent of increase	Competition and Markets Authority findings
Liothyronine A hormone used to treat an underactive thyroid	The NHS spent more than £34 million on Liothyronine in 2016-17 compared with around £600,000 in 2006. The medicine was de-branded in 2007. Concordia, a pharmaceutical company, increased the pack price by almost 6,000% in the 10 years to 2017, while production costs remained broadly stable.	Statement of objection issued in November 2017, alleging that Concordia abused its dominant position to overcharge the NHS.
Hydrocortisone A steroid used to treat adrenal insufficiency, for example due to Addison's disease	Actavis UK, a pharmaceutical company, increased the price of 10mg and 20mg packs of hydrocortisone tablets by 12,000% and 9,500% respectively between April 2008 and March 2016, compared with the branded version of the medicine which was sold by a different company before April 2008.	Statement of objection issued in December 2016, alleging that Actavis UK had breached competition law by charging excessive and unfair prices in the UK.
Phenytoin sodium An anti-epileptic medicine	Prices increased overnight in September 2012 after the medicine was de-branded. As a result of these increases, NHS expenditure on phenytoin sodium capsules increased from about £2 million a year in 2012 to about £50 million in 2013.	Infringement decision, following a statement of objection in 2015, announced in December 2016. The Authority found that the two pharmaceutical companies involved, Pfizer and Flynn, had abused their dominant positions by imposing unfair prices for phenytoin sodium capsules. It imposed a financial penalty of £84.2 million on Pfizer and £5.2 million on Flynn and directed both companies to reduce their prices. Both Pfizer and Flynn appealed the Competition and Markets Authority's findings to the Competition Appeals Tribunal and the judgment is awaited at the time of writing.

Source: National Audit Office

3.14 The Act also provides the legal basis for price control of other types of medicines called 'specials'. Specials are unlicensed medicines manufactured to meet the needs of individual patients, for example liquid forms of medicines for patients unable to swallow tablets. Around 250 high-volume and high-cost specials are included in the Drug Tariff, making up 29% of spend on specials in 2016-17. For these, pharmacy contractors are reimbursed a set price, based on a selection of manufacturers' prices. For specials not in the Drug Tariff, pharmacy contractors are reimbursed at the invoice price or cost of the ingredients.

3.15 The Department will have new powers to obtain information about the cost of medicines, which are due to come into force from July 2018. The 2017 Act makes it mandatory for suppliers of medicines to provide regular information on sales. The associated draft regulations also include a requirement for companies to notify the Department of any supply issues, or plans to discontinue supply. The Department also expects to have the power to request additional information within two working days, as required, to support the concessionary price setting process and in relation to medicine supply disruptions. However, these new powers are untested and the Department will need sufficient resources to implement them.

Appendix One

Our investigative approach

Scope

1 This investigation sets out the facts in relation to the increase in prices of certain generic medicines during 2017-18 and the impact on clinical commissioning groups' expenditure. It covers:

- NHS spending on generic medicines;
- possible causes of the price increases in the market for generic medicines; and
- how the Department of Health & Social Care (the Department) and its arm's-length bodies responded to the price increases.

2 We carried out our investigation between January and April 2018.

Methods

3 We reviewed policy documents, guidance, reports and meeting minutes from the Department, NHS England, the Medicines and Healthcare products Regulatory Agency and the NHS Business Services Authority. We also reviewed reports and analysis by other organisations including the Organisation for Economic Co-operation and Development.

4 We analysed primary care prescribing data (ePACT2, published by NHS Business Services Authority), Drug Tariff data published by OpenPrescribing.net, and the Department's published price concessions to understand expenditure on medicines and quantify the net spend on concessionary prices. We also analysed Prescription Cost Analysis data, published by the NHS Business Services Authority, to understand volume and trends. For requests for concessionary prices we analysed data provided by the Pharmaceutical Services Negotiating Committee.

5 We interviewed officials from the Department who have a role in setting medicines policy, the reimbursement system and ensuring continuity of supply. We interviewed officials from NHS England and NHS Improvement to establish the wider impact and their respective roles and responsibilities. We also interviewed officials from the Medicines and Healthcare products Regulatory Agency, which regulates the medicines market, and the NHS Business Services Authority, which administers the reimbursement process.

6 We conducted three case study visits, visiting clinical commissioning groups and one acute NHS foundation trust. These were selected to represent a mix of urban/rural areas, regions and average per person spend on medicines. The visits provided contextual information, which helped further direct our inquiries.

7 We spoke to staff from a range of organisations to seek their views on the market for generic medicines, including the recent price increases of certain medicines. The organisations we interviewed, or received written evidence from, were:

- **national bodies:** British Association of Dermatologists; Competition and Markets Authority; Dispensing Doctors' Association; NHS Clinical Commissioners; Pharmaceutical Services Negotiating Committee; Royal College of General Practitioners; Royal College of Physicians;

- **pharmaceutical industry:** Association of the British Pharmaceutical Industry; British Generic Manufacturers Association; Healthcare Distribution Association; and

- **other:** All-Party Parliamentary Group on Pharmacy; OpenPrescribing, Evidence-Based Medicine DataLab at the University of Oxford; and PrescQIPP.

Made in the USA
Monee, IL
05 November 2026

67386678R00017